1,000,000 Books

are available to read at

Forgotten Books

www.ForgottenBooks.com

Read online
Download PDF
Purchase in print

ISBN 978-1-332-96225-9
PIBN 10443648

This book is a reproduction of an important historical work. Forgotten Books uses state-of-the-art technology to digitally reconstruct the work, preserving the original format whilst repairing imperfections present in the aged copy. In rare cases, an imperfection in the original, such as a blemish or missing page, may be replicated in our edition. We do, however, repair the vast majority of imperfections successfully; any imperfections that remain are intentionally left to preserve the state of such historical works.

Forgotten Books is a registered trademark of FB &c Ltd.
Copyright © 2018 FB &c Ltd.
FB &c Ltd, Dalton House, 60 Windsor Avenue, London, SW19 2RR.
Company number 08720141. Registered in England and Wales.

For support please visit www.forgottenbooks.com

1 MONTH OF FREE READING

at

www.ForgottenBooks.com

By purchasing this book you are eligible for one month membership to ForgottenBooks.com, giving you unlimited access to our entire collection of over 1,000,000 titles via our web site and mobile apps.

To claim your free month visit: www.forgottenbooks.com/free443648

* Offer is valid for 45 days from date of purchase. Terms and conditions apply.

English
Français
Deutsche
Italiano
Español
Português

www.forgottenbooks.com

Mythology Photography **Fiction**
Fishing Christianity **Art** Cooking
Essays Buddhism Freemasonry
Medicine **Biology** Music **Ancient
Egypt** Evolution Carpentry Physics
Dance Geology **Mathematics** Fitness
Shakespeare **Folklore** Yoga Marketing
Confidence Immortality Biographies
Poetry **Psychology** Witchcraft
Electronics Chemistry History **Law**
Accounting **Philosophy** Anthropology
Alchemy Drama Quantum Mechanics
Atheism Sexual Health **Ancient History**
Entrepreneurship Languages Sport
Paleontology Needlework Islam
Metaphysics Investment Archaeology
Parenting Statistics Criminology
Motivational

NOTICES

OF

THE MOST REMARKABLE FIRES

IN EDINBURGH,

FROM 1385 TO 1824,

INCLUDING AN ACCOUNT

OF THE

GREAT FIRE OF NOVEMBER, 1824.

By ROBERT CHAMBERS,

EDITOR OF "TRADITIONS OF EDINBURGH."

Printed for CHAS. SMITH & Co. *Hanover Street,*
EDINBURGH.

1824.

9466.28.5
B 9507.10

Cochrane Gift

James Clarke & Co. Printers,
High Street, Edinburgh.

PREFACE.

I cannot give this little pamphlet to the world, without regretting, that the extreme haste with which its materials were thrown together, has prevented me from making it so perfect in every respect, as I had designed. One or two instances of destructive fires are omitted in the series, such as that of Martin's Printing-House in St. John's Hill, which took place about forty years ago, and completely laid waste the celebrated Apollo Press, (by which BELL's *beautiful edition of the* BRITISH POETS *was printed,) besides scorching to death several horses in the stables underneath. Other important conflagrations do not receive their due share of attention; and too little notice is taken of the causes of the various fires, and the methods taken to prevent and suppress them. Such* omissions, *however, form the least faults of the work; for I am afraid that it contains greater faults of* commission. *Quaint, local, and old-fashioned forms of expression abound. Yet, perhaps these were in a great measure unavoidable, in the course of hurried transcriptions from antiquated documents; and, as for such words as* land, flat, *and* close, *I sincerely believe that, being so appropriate to the localities described, they would have been ill exchanged for any English synonymes whatever. I have endeavoured to enliven the subject as much as possible, by occasional anecdotes which I had hoarded for other purposes, with the view to make the work interesting to a more extensive class than those who read for mere information. The object which has actuated me in this, as well as in the haste of my collections, may be an atonement for all errors—a desire of adding a drop to that stream of charity, which is now flowing so unsparingly to the relief of the unfortunate.*

ROBERT CHAMBERS.

INDIA PLACE, *Nov.* 23, 1824.

REMARKABLE FIRES
IN
EDINBURGH.

1385.—In the early periods of its history, Edinburgh was so much exposed to the ravages of the English, that the Scottish Monarchs seldom resided in it, even after it had become a place of sufficient note and resort for a royal residence. The ancient hereditary enemies of Scotland, in all their incursions across the Border, were in the habit of burning, as well as pillaging the towns on the south side of the Forth; and, we have no doubt, that on such occasions, Edinburgh suffered its full share of the calamities attendant upon these disastrous wars. It was partly destroyed, in 1385, when Richard II. invaded Scotland with a numerous army, and ravaged many of the southern counties. On the approach of the Duke of Lancaster, with the first division of this formidable host, the citizens used the precaution of removing their effects, and unroofing their houses, which, being at that period covered with straw, would have fallen an easy prey to the flames. The Duke forbore to do any injury to the city, on account of the hospitable reception which he had met with some time before from the monks of Holyrood. But when the king arrived in person, with the chief portion of the army, less mercy was shown. It was immediately after this calamity, that Robert II. gave the citizens permission to build houses within the limits of the castle, with no other proviso than that they should be persons of good fame,—a privilege of which advantage does not appear to have been taken to any great extent, though it was calculated to secure them from the depredations and cruelty of their enemies.

1528.—The Monastery of Blackfriars,* situated upon the spot where the High School now stands, was burnt down.

* This celebrated religious establishment was founded in 1230, by Alexander II. After the above disas-

1544.—This year was rendered one of the most disastrous Scotland ever saw, by an invasion of the English, and the conflagration of Edinburgh. After the death of James V. in 1542, Henry VIII. impressed by views of policy which had moved even his remote predecessor Edward I. entered into a negotiation with the Scottish Regency, the object of which was, to obtain the infant Mary as a wife for his son; but, from the want of patience and faith which he manifested, the Scotch considered themselves justifiable in breaking off the match. The King of England, however, resolving to accomplish by force what he could not attain by peaceable means, sent the Earl of Hertford with a fleet and a large army, " to let the Scots see," says an old historian, " what they were to expect if they did not speedily resolve upon the treaty." The Earl landed at Granton Grange, two miles west from Leith,

ter, it was scarcely rebuilt at the Reformation, when the ecclesiastics were stripped of their property. It was formerly denominated *Mansif Regis*, having been the abode of the king. The church of St. Mary in the Fields, and the gardens belonging to its provost and prebendaries, all of which were connected with this monastery, occupied the whole district south of the Cowgate, between the Pleasance and the Potterrow.

took that town without difficulty, and then marched directly to Edinburgh, of which he became master with the same ease. The castle alone was not delivered up, and it was not judged necessary to besiege it; but the city was given up to pillage, and then to the flames,* which are said by Lindsay to have destroyed " the town with all the kirkis thereof;" † though we are inclined to believe that

* " And finally, it was determyned by the sayde Lorde Lieutenaunt, vtterly to ruynate and destroye the sayde towne with fyer; which, for that the nyghte drewe faste on, we omytted thoroughly to execute on that daye; but settynge fyer in thre or iiii partes of the towne, we repayred for that nighte into our campe, and the nexte mornynge very erly we began where we lefte, and continued burnynge all that daye, and the two dayes nexte ensuinge contynually, so that neyther within ye waules, nor in the suburbes, was lefte any one house vnbrent, besydes the innumerable botyes, poyles and pillages, that our souldyours brought fro thense, notwithstanding habundance whiche was consumed with fyer. Also we brent thabbey called Holy Rodehouse, and the pallice adioynynge to the same."— See " *the late Expedicion into Sootlande, made by the Kinges Hyhnys Armye, Vnder the conduit of the Ryght Honorable the Earl of Hertforde, the xere of our Lorde God* 1544. *Londini. &c.*" in " Dalyell's Fragments of Scottish History."

† Cronicles, vol. ii. p. 417.

the calamity was not so general or so destructive as the preceding authorities would seem to indicate. *

1572.—A shot fired from the castle set fire to a corn stack in the Canongate; a curious cir-

* Before the burning of Edinburgh in 1544, we cannot imagine the houses to have been very fine, or their accommodations convenient; the following being a description of the country residences of the most powerful noblemen in the year immediately preceding:
Sir Ralph Sadler, the English ambassador, writes to the ministry of his own country: " I hade leuir be among the Turkis; for in my L. of Angus house, wher he is, I cannot be, the same being (as I am crediblye informed) in such ruyne, as he hethe there scant one chalmer for himeselfe and my Ladye his wife; and lykeways my L. L. of Cassillis and Glencairne which dwell xx myllis a sondir, and almost xxx myllis from my L. of Anguse, be not so well housed as they can spare me any lodginge; for undoubtedly the l. l. houses in this miserable and beggarlye cuntrie, be not efter such sorte as in uther cuntries." *Sadler's Embassies, MS. Adv. Lib. A. II.* 21. p. 313.
It is, however, material to observe, that as the Scots were then apprehending invasion from England, they might make themselves appear as poor as possible, so as to make an invasion seem to the ambassador " not worth the while."

cumstance, which denotes the rarity of buildings at that time in the Court end of the town.

1573.—On the 12th of February, a great fire took place under the following circumstances:—Kirkaldy of Grange held out the castle for Queen Mary's interest, and had many contentions with the troops of the King, her infant son. " On the morning of the day above mentioned," says an old chronicler *, " the soldiers of the castle set fire to two thatched houses† in the Castle-wynd, when, the wind blowing vehemently from the west, the conflagration increased, and continued from house to house till it came to Forrester's Wynd ‡, whair, by providence, it stayit, notwithstanding the grit schoting of the castle." Many people were rendered destitute by means of this wide and dreadful devastation; and their misery was increased by the soldiers from the castle issuing out and carrying off their effects, which they had deposited for security in the streets.

* Bannatyne, " *Journal of Transactions in Scotland,* 1571-2-3-4."
† A few houses still remain in the Castle Wynd, north side of the Grass-market, covered, in the primeval style, with thatch.
‡ First alley eastward from Libberton's Wynd.

1585.—In December, 1585, a destructive fire broke out in Peebles's Wynd, (where Blair Street is now situated,) by which the citizens were greatly alarmed, and the conflagration of the whole neighbourhood for some time apprehended. It was occasioned by a baker's boy, who, either from accident or design, set fire to a stack of peats belonging to his master. "Edinburgh," says Maitland, " was at this time greatly pestered with stacks of heather, broom, whins, and other fuel, erected in closes and wynds, to the great discontent of the people, and danger of the neighbourhood;" which at once indicates that the *closes* of Edinburgh could then afford room for piles which they could not in later times accommodate, and that coals were not, at the period mentioned, in general use. The unfortunate boy, who caused the burning, met with a severity of punishment highly disproportioned to his offence, being burnt quick at the cross next day. The custom of heaping up fuel within the city was abolished by an edict of the Town-council.

1601.—" The 5 day of August, at euin, ane house brunt at the Canagaitt fit, besyde the grass crosse."—*Birrel's Diary*, p. 55.

1603.—"The 8 of Januar, certain stebillis and houses brunt at the Netherbow, on the north syde of the gaite besyde the Netherbow Port, occupyit by James Wright, stabler."—*Ibid.* p. 57.

1661.—A great fire occurred in the Pleasance. *Council Register*, vol. xx. p. 227.

1670.—*Hugh Boyd's Land* [qu?] was burnt down, and a collection made at the kirk-doors in his behalf. *Ibid.*

1674.—*John Handaside's Land* [qu?] burnt down. A reward was appointed to be given to those who had been active in extinguishing the flames, and a collection made for the relief of the sufferers. An act was also made, exempting the persons burnt out from paying any rent for the half-year during which the fire occurred. *Ibid.*

1676.—A fire occurred at the entry into the Parliament Close. Acts were passed for the removal of the rubbish, which for some time interrupted the street and entry. The tenements which were burnt in June 1824 seem to have been then erected; and, though the fire of 1700 involved this district, it is probable that the walls survived, and were of the age we mention. In consequence of this fire, there were numerous acts for the prevention and suppression of future fires, and for building houses of stone instead of wood, and covering them with slate instead of thatch.

1680.—A fire occurred in the West Bow, when the house of Sir John Nisbet, then King's Advocate, was burnt. The Town-council, probably from a mean motive, compensated the damage of his property by a *douceur* of £1000 *Scots*. By an act of Council, passed in 1659, fires were prohibited to be kept in the shops and booths of the West Bow.—A curious circumstance took place in the West Bow, about a century ago. The ancestor of the present proprietor of Vogrie, who made a fortune and bought that property, was a shopkeeper in this ancient street. He one day sent his female servant down to the cellar for some article, of which he wanted a supply for the shop. The girl took a candle with her, which, while providing what she was in quest of, she placed in the mouth of an open barrel, among what she supposed to be leek-seed; and, coming away with her hands engaged, left it there, burning. On ascending to the shop, her master inquired what she had done with the candle. She trivially mentioned the place where she had placed it. Mr. Dewar was horror-struck—the barrel contained gunpowder! However, with a degree of courage and presence of mind, which we cannot too highly admire, he went down to the cellar, approached the barrel, and, spreading his hands like the basin of a night-candlestick, beneath the light, in order to catch any sparks that might fall, brought it away! In performing this daring and dexterous exploit, his face for a moment overhung the very mouth of the barrel. Had but a spark fallen, he must have been blown into atoms, and the West Bow would have now been very different from what it is!

1690.—A fire in Provost Stewart's Close. Collections made for the sufferers. *Council Register,* vol. xxxiii. p. 140.

1691.—A fire at the Netherbow Port. *Qu.*—could this be one of the burnings alluded to in the notes to "Rokeby?"

1696.—The Schoolmaster's house in the Canongate brunt down,—in consequence of which there was an act of Council, enabling the sufferer to take up a school in the City.

1698.—A fire in the College Wynd.

1700.—In the last year of the century, at a time when Scotland was suffering under all the horrors of famine, a most calamitous fire broke out in Edinburgh. It was on Saturday, the memorable 3d of February, that this awful disaster, which made such a noise at the time, and was afterwards so well remembered, took place. The flames broke out, about eleven o'clock at night, in the north-east corner of the Meal Market, a small court of buildings then chiefly occupied by lawyers, situated upon the north side of the Cowgate, immediately behind the Parliament Close. From this spot the fire spread up the hill to the Parliament Close, destroying all the buildings called Kirk-heugh, which was then a sort of shoe-market, and at length reached the High Street, where some houses contiguous to the cross were involved in the general ruin. Previous to this event, the tenements upon the south side of the Parliament Close were fifteen storeys in height, as viewed from Kirk-heugh behind; but, on being rebuilt, were curtailed of at least three floors, and, at their late destruction in 1824, were only eleven storeys above the ground, exclusive of garrets. We think it necessary to be thus minute, as many misapprehensions and exaggerations have been entertained respecting the height of these houses, which were always said to be thirteen or fourteen storeys; whereas they have not been more than eleven, since the burning of 1700. They were always pointed out as the highest in Edinburgh.

The Parliament Close was all rebuilt in a uniform style of architecture, and, till the erection of the New Town, was by far the most splendid piece of building in the city. Maitland, the elaborate and accurate, though somewhat magniloquent historian of Edinburgh, lavishes much praise upon the buildings, and calls them palaces with fronts of marble. Whether or not they deserved his commendations, it might have been disputed, even in 1824, if the New Town contained any edifices equal to them in massive and picturesque magnificence.

We propose to continue the history of this remarkable fire, by a series of interesting extracts from contemporary writers, and the narratives of eye-witnesses. The following letter from Mr. Duncan Forbes, (father of the celebrated President,) to his brother, Colonel Forbes, contains a very lively and picturesque account of the event :—

"Dear Brother, *My last was with humbling news, and this with news more humbling. Upon Saturday night, by ten o'clock, a fire broke out in Mr. John Buchan's closet-window, towards the Meal Market. It continued till eleven o'clock of the day with the greatest fervour *(frayor)* and vehemency that ever I saw fire do, notwithstanding that I saw London burn.

"There are burnt, by the easiest computation, between three and four hundred families; all the pride of Edinburgh is sunk; from the Cowgate to the High Street all is burnt, and hardly one stone is left upon another. The Commissioner, the President of Parliament, the President of the Court of Session,†

---

* We have taken the liberty of modernizing the orthography of the letter.

† Sir Hugh Dalrymple, son of the first Earl of Stair. The President's Stairs, on the east side of the Parliament Close, derived their name from him. He lived in the fourth flat, which he had insured in the Friendly Office; and, what is very remarkable, the recent de-

the Bank, most of the Lords, lawyers, and clerks, were all burnt, besides many poor and great families. * It is said just now by Sir John Cochran and Jordanhill, that there is more rent burnt in this fire than the whole city of Glasgow will amount to. † The Parliament House very nearly escaped ;‡ all Registers confounded; Clerks' Chambers and processes in such a confusion, that the Lords and Officers of State are just now met in Ross's

struction of this property was compensated upon that very insurance, which had been continued nearly a century.

* The Parliament Close, and the tenements behind, were then the chief residences of the great, and of the highest official characters in the town. The Bank of Scotland, then the only one in the kingdom, which had been instituted only five years before this period, was in the Parliament Close, and burnt out on this occasion, though—as we learn from a scarce pamphlet-history of the establishment,—all the effects, books, and notes, were saved from the flames.—The great Earl of Bute was born (1713) in the Parliament Close.

† This seems scarcely credible.

‡ Had not the wind providentially blown from the south-west, the Parliament House, and all the valuable property therewith connected, must have been destroyed.

Tavern,* in order to adjourn the Session by reason of the disorder. Few people are lost, if any at all: but there was neither heart nor hand left among them for saving from the fire, nor a drop of water in the cisterns. Twenty thousand hands flitting (removing) their trash they knew not where, and hardly twenty at work. These Babels, of ten and fourteen storey high, are down to the ground, and their fall is very terrible. Many rueful spectacles, such as Corserig† naked, with a child under his oxter, hopping for his life. The Fish Market, and all from the Cowgate to Pett Street's Close brunt: the Exchange, vaults, and coal-cellars under the Parliament Close, are still burning. This epitome of dissolution, I send to you, without saying any more, but that the Lord is angry with us, and I see no intercessor. Your loving brother to serve you,

"D. Forbes."

* Andrew Ross kept a tavern in the Exchange buildings, at the head of the Back Stairs, during the early part of the last century. He is mentioned in Pitcairn's Latin poem "*Ad Advenas*," where his face is called "vultus astrifer," in compliment to its pimples. We cannot point out the situation of his tavern at the time of the fire.

† David Home, a Lord of Session, appointed at the Revolution. *See Lord Hailes' Catalogue.*

We extract the following poetical account of the event, from a little pamphlet in two leaves, printed at Edinburgh immediately after the disaster. The poem, which is about twice the length of our extract, is entitled,—" The Dreadful Voice of Fire, begun at Edinburgh the 3d of February, 1700."

* * * * * * * *

" In *Rob'son's Land*, 'bout Ten a cloak at Night,
Happ'ned a Fire, soon shining clear and bright;
And in a Trice, from *North-East*, did o'erspread,
The Fabrick whole, well covered with Lead;
And as if pincht in narrow bounds it went,
Straight for *St. Geil's*; but soon it did repent,
And stayed at the *Statue*, thence did flee
North ward to th' *Croce*, to serve its Luxury.
How it did Triumph o'er the sturdy Oak?
And did obscure fair Cynthia, by its smoak?
Dislodging soon the loving Man and Wife,
The Family and Children, without strife;
From Babel's Tow'rs them sending to the deep
Of saddest Plight, yea some amidst their sleep.
Vulcan was now inexorable grown;
Nor Piety nor Riches would he oune:
Best Gifts of Heav'n and Earth he did disdain,
Threatening with blood, his Fury to maintain;
And deaf as *Adria*, did neglect the Cryes,
Of rich and poor, all in deep Miseryes;
Yea did invade the day of *Holy Rest*,
And so the Toun, with hideous flames, molest.

He raged so, so domineered he,
As, but himself, no other god could be.
At last, by Holy Pray'rs he was appeas'd,
And then his force and cruel fury ceas'd.
Hence learn, ye Mortals, what great Madness be,
To build up houses thrice five stories high,
Or to put Trust in any Earthly Thing,
Save in Great GOD, of Heav'n and Earth the King;
But trust in him alone, who can defend
You, from sad accidents, and dreadful end ;
And now repent, and to the Lord now turn,
Lest he should you, in Flames eternal, burn."

Patrick Walker, well known to stall students for his biographies of the *Martyrs*, in his *Life and Prophecies of Mr. Daniel Cargill*, after detailing the miseries endured in the country, by famine, in 1700, has the following remarks upon the fire of the Parliament Close. " I cannot pass this occasion of giving remarks upon some observable providences that followed these strange judgments, upon persons who dwelt in low-lying fertile places, who laid themselves out to raise markets when at such a height, and had little sympathy with the poor, or those who lived in cold muirish places, who thought those who lived in fertile places had a little heaven: But, soon after, their little heavens were turned into little hells, by unexpected providences. Some wrote Sixteen Remarks upon that terrible fire which fell out on the 2d and 3d of February 1700, in the Parliament Close in Edinburgh; one was, that it was most of those people who dwelt there were rich, and lived sumptuously and had little sympathy with the distressed case of the land *: but their fine houses,

---

* The miseries of that dreadful period were perhaps beyond all that ever happened in any country upon similar occasions. Traditions are still preserved in some districts respecting the cold, famine, and mortality of the period. For several years before 1700, the seasons had been so severe, that the feathered creation decayed, and insects, such as flies, were almost extirpated. Many people lost the use of their feet and hands, from reaping amidst the snow, which almost buried the crop. Meal became so scarce, that it was sold, when to be got at all, at two shillings per peck, a vast price in those days. When markets were exhausted, the poor women, who chanced to come too late, were to be seen clapping their hands and tearing the clothes off their heads, with the most vehement and heart-rending exclamations. In Ayrshire, if not also in other districts, the farmers were in the habit of grinding a small proportion of corn with way-side herbs and seeds of the most disgusting and unwholesome nature, so as to make up a sufficient quantity of *parritch* or *cakes* for a meal; and bleeding the cattle for nutriment was also common in that part of the country. Deaths and burials were so frequent, that

which were eleven years in building, were, in a few hours, turned to a burnt ruinous heap."

The following curious document is selected from a small volume, published in 1714, containing the principal acts of Parliament, Assembly, and Town-Council, respecting the suppression of Sabbath-breaking, Vice, and Immorality:

"*Act anent suppressing* IMMORALITIES, *to be read every Council-day, after Whitsunday and Martinmas.*

"*Edinburgh, December* 4, 1702.

" The which day, the Lord Provost, Baillies, Council, and Deacons of the Crafts, considering the great growth of immoralities within the City and Suburbs, and the fearful Re-

the living were wearied with taking care of the dead; and it was difficult to raise a sufficient company for such a purpose: many corpses got neither coffin nor winding sheet, but were drawn to the grave upon sledges, as is done upon occasions of pestilence abroad. The affections of domestic life disappeared in the selfishness of individual misery; and some declared that they could mind nothing but food, and were " utterly unconcerned about their souls, whether they went to heaven or hell."

bukes of God, by a dreadful Fire in the Parliament Close, Kirkheugh, and Cowgate, which happened about mid-night, upon the 3d February, 1700, and which is recorded in the Council-Books, with their Christian Sentiments thereanent, upon the 24th of April thereafter.

" As also, remembering the terrible Fire which happened on the north side of the Lawnmarket, about mid-day, upon the 28th of October, 1701, wherein several Men, Women, and Children, were consumed in the Flames, and lost by the fall of ruinous walls: And further, remembering that most tremendous and terrible blowing up of gun-powder in Leith, upon the 3d of July last, wherein sundry persons were lost, and wonderful ruins made in the place; and likewise reflecting upon other Tokens of God's wrath lately come upon us, and what we are more and more threatened with, being moved with the zeal of God, and the tyes he hath laid on us, and that we have taken upon ourselves, to appear for him in our several stations, do, in the Lord's strength, resolve to be more watchful over our hearts and ways than formerly: And each of us, in our several capacities, to reprove vice with that due zeal and prudence, as we shall have occasion, and to endeavour to promote the vigorous execution of those good laws made for suppressing of vice, and punishing the vitious, &c. * * * under the penalty of Twenty Merks Scots, *toties quoties*," &c.

Perhaps the most remarkable feature in the history of this dreadful calamity, was the superstitious belief, entertained by the vulgar and fostered by their rulers and teachers, that the whole was what they called *a judgment* of the Almighty, to punish them for their sins, and warn them to repentance. This notion, absurd as it may seem, was warmly taken up by the preachers of the day, and made the subject of several sermons, edicts, and advices. Some of these documents are exceedingly curious, and give a lively picture of the state of the public mind at the beginning of the eighteenth century. The following extracts, while they record several historical incidents not yet noticed, will, we hope, be found interesting from the above reason.

The Reverend Robert Scott, D.D. minister of the New North Church, published, in 1701, "*A Sermon upon occasion of the late* DREADFUL FIRE, *which happened*," &c. &c. of which the following passages are worthy of notice:

" Sure I am, the last of these (*calamities, alluding to the burning of Gomorrah*,) has sadly overtaken our Metropolis of this kingdom, and even the beauty and glory of that city, the most stately edifices, (the palaces and particular undertakings of princes being laid aside,) we may say, in all the Christian or Pagan world*. We are not so peevish [as] to account, with some, either the building of them so lofty, or the furnishing of them so richly, a sin: No, it was one of the blessings that Almighty God beautified the reign of Solomon with, even wealth and national glory." * * *

" *** To return to our own ruines, in the sight of that terrible conflagration, were not the hearts of people generally like to melt within them? Or, if any were under an obduration of spirit, they suffered under a greater plague than that of burning. Who could think of so swift a misery, and so wasting a stroke upon his neighbours, and not be afflicted with the deepest anguish of soul? Or who could look upon the mighty hand of God, raining fire in all the corners of the city, as if the infernal lake had been broke open, or God had given

---

* Another proof of the esteem in which these buildings were held.

commission to the pure element, by which he shall burn up the earth and the works thereof at the final overthrow of the world? I say, who can yet make but a reflex thought upon that terrible visitation from heaven, and not be engaged into the deepest seriousness." The sermon is concluded with a hint towards the propriety of erecting a monument, similar to that of London, commemorative of the fire in the Parliament Close.

In Willison's "*Treatise on the Sanctification of the Lord's Day,*" among a long list of judgments executed upon Sabbath-breakers, we find the following passage: "Likewise in Edinburgh, where Sabbath-breaking very much abounded, (as appears by the acts of Assembly made against that sin,) the fairest and stateliest of its buildings, in the Parliament Close and about it, (to which scarce any in Britain were comparable,) were, on the fourth of February, (being the Lord's Day) burnt down, and laid in ashes and ruins in the space of a few hours, to the astonishment and terror of the sorrowful inhabitants, whereof I myself was an eye-witness; and the effects of that fire are visible to this day. Yea, so great was the terror and confusion of that Lord's day, that the people of the city were in no case to attend any sermon or public worship upon it, though there was a great number of worthy ministers convened in the place (beside the reverend ministers of the city) ready to have prayed with or preached to the people on that sad occasion, for the General Assembly was sitting there at the time; but the dismal state of the city made this impracticable. However, the Lord himself, by that silent Sabbath, did loudly preach to all the inhabitants of the city, &c."

In the " *Memoirs, or Spiritual Exercises of Elizabeth Wast; written by her own hand—Edinburgh,* 1733," we find the following remarkable passage: " About this time, there happened a very lamentable Providence in the City. The 3d day of February, about Ten at Night, a fire broke out in the Meal-Market, the like of which, I believe, was not seen in many Generations: it burnt so vehemently that it was thought the most Part of the City, would been consumed; the Flames were so terrible that none durst come near to quench it: It was also a very great Wind, which blew to such a Degree, that, with the sparks that came from the Fire, there was nothing to be seen through the whole City, but as it had been Showers of Fire like Showers of Snow, they were so thick; it was to me as an Emblem of Hell, and oftentimes Sodom came in my Mind that Night. O but it was a sad and lamentable Sight to look upon, to see the most populous Place in the City (the Parliament-close) in a red Flame, the Flames flying in the Elements, and no Hands endeavouring to put them out! There was much of God to be seen in this Fire; for he gave Warning of it before it came. Sabbath before this, there was such a Smell of burning, that those in the Meal-market, Kirk-heugh, and the Parliament-close, went from House to House, to see if there was any Thing like Fire among them; but none could be found; and this broke out the Saturday following: And, for my own Part, a considerable time before this, I had such *Impressions of Fire* upon my Spirit, that sleeping or waking it was with me; and that Word accompanied my fears, *The Sun rose fair on Sodom that day it was destroyed.* But, passing this, there were some things very remarkable in this Fire: First, it began in his *land* who gave the Covenant to the Hangman out of his own hand to be burnt,* being youngest Baillie

---

* This is perhaps connected with a tradition, which was revived upon the second burning of this district,

in that Time; and it was very observable, he had never the Use of his Hand as formerly, after that time: And now God in his Providence hath sent a Burning among his *Lands*,

and continued for some days current among the lower classes. This far we know, and can authenticate, that Mrs. Martin, the venerable and well-remembered landlady of a tavern at the foot of the Covenant Close,—in which it has always been said that the Covenant was placed for signatures, in 1640,—in pointing out the scene of that remarkable event, used to tell her guests, that the house had been twice burnt since the time of the Covenant, and that it was destined *yet another time* to suffer the same fate, according to a prediction which many believed. Whether the house was twice burnt before Mrs. Martin's time, or whether such a prediction was ever made, we cannot determine; but certain it is, that, in the fire of November 1824, it suffered so much as nearly to verify the aged tavern-keeper's tale. The house alluded to was, about the middle of the last century, and till within the last forty years, one of the most respectable residences in Edinburgh. In 1754, the upper flat was possessed jointly by Messrs. Macqueen and Veitch, afterwards better known as Lords Braxfield and Elliock. At a somewhat later period, that distinguished orator and dignified judge, Lord Alemoor, lived in the first flat above the tavern; and Murray of Cherrytrees possessed the floor above. For further particulars, see " *Traditions of Edinburgh*," No. II. p. 186.

so that that which was eleven years a-building was not six Hours of burning: Notwithstanding this, he was a good Man, and lamented to his Death the burning the Covenant; he was also very helpful to the Lord's Prisoners, during the late Persecution: Yet it was well observed by one, *As Burning was the Sin, so Burning was the Punishment.* 2dly, It was observed, That, as it began in his *Land* who burnt the Covenant, so it never rested till it came to the Place where it was burnt, and there it stayed without any Cause whatsoever;* but it had its commission from the Lord, *Hitherto shall ye come and no further.* This opened the Mouth of both Good and Bad, to express, *O the burnt Covenant! O the burnt Covenant! This is come upon us for burning of the Covenant.* 3dly, It is very observable, That the Fire did resemble *the Fire of the late Persecution*, kindled by a Prelatick Party against the Presbyterians, in these four respects: * * * * * the most Part of them that suffered at this Fire

* We apprehend, that after it had burnt its way to the Cross, where the Covenant in 1661 met with its fate, the interval between the south and north sides of the High Street might be a sufficient bar to its further progress.

were rich People.　　*　　*　　*　　*
I cannot tell what Effect this Dispensation had upon my Spirit; I thought it dang me stupid and senseless in the time of it, so that I could not so much as pour out a Prayer for the quenching of it."

We will complete the history of this Fire with the act of Council passed upon the occasion :—

" *Edinburgh, the 7th day of February,* 1700.

" The which day, the Council considering the sad and deplorable condition of the neighbourhood of this City, occasioned by the late dreadful fire, that, upon Saturday's night last, about ten of the clock, brock out in the north-east corner of the Meal-mercat, and consumed to ashes all the said mercat, all the statelie buildings of the deceast Baillie Thomas Robertson, on both the sydes of the Kirkheugh, the Exchange, and the whole Parliament Closs, except the Treasury House, which, by great Providence, was preserved, DOE therefore recommend to Baillie Patrick Johnstoun, to call for the Session of the Old Kirk, and to take up a list of the whole families who have suffered by that terrible conflagration, to the effect that the Council may know what persons are liable to sustain their losses, and what not, that some speedie remedie may be taken for their relief, and recommends to the said Baillie to call for the Collector of the Stent, and get ane accompt of the valuation of the whole brunt lands: And, in like manner, the Council recommends to the present Baillies of this City, Canongate, Leith, West Port, Potterrow, and hail Suburbs, to cause the Constables in their bounds to make a diligent search for all abstracted goods, to the effect they may be secured for the right owners: And also the Council recommends to the Dean of Guild, to accommodat those who had shops in the Exchange with Crames in the ordinar places, there to continue for some time during the Council's pleasure: And the Council Doe nominat and appoint Baillie Johnstoun, &c. &c. as a Committee, to enquire into the rise and progress of the said dreadful fire, and how and in what manner the lyke may be prevented in tyme coming," &c. &c. *Council Register, vol.* 36, *p.* 475.

1707.—In November 1707, a fire broke out at the head of the Canongate, of which Elisabeth Wast gives the following account:—

" Another sad and dreadful fire happened that same day eight days, in the Canongate Head, about two in the morning; when the cry arose, I being asleep, got up in haste, and took such a trembling, that I could hardly win to the room-door. We being in the Parliament Closs, when I came to the window, I saw the terrible light; both sides of the Canongate were burning at once. How I was affected on this melancholy sight, none on earth knows, but still I saw the Lord contending with us and against us, (but we could not see,) by doubling the judgments in that place; for mine eyes had seen that same place burnt eleven years before.* O how the Heads and Hands of the Worthies presented me, which had been set upon that Port,† where these flames were flying! these had secret languages to me."

1725.—" At this time, a great fire happened in the Lawn Market. It burned with such rapidity, that neither the household furniture,

---

* In another part of her " Exercises," she makes allusion to a fire which occurred here, three weeks previous to the great fire in the Parliament Close.

* The Netherbow Port.

goods, nor even the merchants' books could be saved from the flames in many of the houses that were consumed. A contribution was set on foot by the Magistrates for relief of the sufferers. £938. 15s. 8d. were raised for this charitable purpose. The sum was distributed by the magistrates and ministers of Edinburgh, and Lord Miltoun. A great part of it was disposed of in this upright and equitable manner!—To one gentleman, afterwards Member of Parliament for the city, £124. 4s.; to another gentleman, afterwards Lord Provost, £225; to a poor Episcopal clergyman, £2." *Arnot's History of Edinburgh*, p. 205.

We have consulted a printed account of the distribution of the above charity, and find that to Mr James Kerr, goldsmith, was allotted £120. 4s. 0½d.; to James Lind, merchant, £225; and to Mr George Honeyman, £2. These various gentlemen were the Member of Parliament, Lord Provost, and Episcopal clergyman, mentioned by Mr Arnot. In this list it is remarkable that Colonel Francis Charteris*

---

* Though this notorious personage was oftener than once tried in the Court of Justiciary, and has been held up to contempt by both painters and poets, he was not in reality so bad a man as he has been represented. The virtuous President Forbes, in his letters, calls him his

subscribed £4. 4s. and was the only individual, distinct from Churches and Societies, who subscribed any sum.—John Dun, writer, " who suffered at the late fire at the Bow-head," received £25 from the Charity.

1739.—The great storm of wind which occurred on the 14th of January this year, occasioned two destructive fires in opposite quarters of the town—one in a brewery at the east end of Hope Park, another in a farm-house belonging to one Mrs. Angus, near Canonmills. A particular account of this memorable storm, by which many houses were beaten down, and the leads blown off the house in the Parliament Close, will be found in *" A Tour through Great Britain, by a Gentleman, 1748, vol. iv. p. 94.*

1755.—" In the morning of May 2,* between twelve and one o'clock, a dreadful fire broke out in a *land* opposite to the foot of Martin's Wynd, (where the South Bridge now stands,)

" worthy friend ;" and Sir Walter Scott has written, " Whatever might be Charteris' general character, the charge of rape was an atrocious attempt to levy money from him by terror." *Quar. Rev. of Culloden Papers*, Jan. 1816, p. 318.
* Scots Mag. May, 1755.

which entirely consumed that *land*, and threatened the neighbourhood with destruction. The fire had come to so great a height before it was discovered, that the inhabitants, with difficulty, escaped with their lives, and lost their effects of every kind. The working people, on hearing the fire-drum, suspected it to be a stratagem used by the press-gang, who had used such an one some time before at Leith: and, therefore, sufficient help was not so speedily got as usual in such cases. The principal sufferer was Mr. James Stirling,* who, in goods and furniture, exclusive of clothes, account-books, and smaller articles, was supposed to have lost about £1600. A subscription was enthusiastically entered into, in behalf of this respectable citizen, and the other sufferers; and the Sun Fire Office of London transmitted Five Guineas to their agent in Edinburgh†, to be distributed among the firemen, and such other individuals as had ex-

* Mr. Stirling's shop in the Cowgate was, about the middle of the last century, one of the most respectable in the city. Tickets for the Concert, Assembly, &c. were usually sold at it; and it was considered a good place for hanging up a subscription-paper of any kind.

† An agent, deputed from this office, in 1733, was the first appearance of an insurance office in Edinburgh.

erted themselves most upon the calamitous occasion."

1758.—On the 12th of August, between nine and ten o'clock forenoon, a dreadful fire broke out in a cabinet-maker's warehouse, in Carrubber's Close, which, before any assistance could be got, involved the whole in a flame, burst through the roof, and spread to the adjoining tenements. For ten hours, the flames raged uncontrolled; but, by the use of several fire-engines, and the attention of the civil authorities, were at length suppressed. Very great damage was done, four houses being altogether destroyed, with all they contained.

1771.—A tenement, called *Buchanan's Land*, at the head of the Old Bank Close, one of those which had been burnt in 1725, or rather a fabric built upon its site, took fire on Saturday the 25th of January, 1771. The flames were first discovered by some soldiers in the Castle, who instantly gave the alarm. They originated in a garret, occupied by the servants of General Lockhart of Carnwath, whose house was the second *flat* of this *land*. Mr. Ilay Campbell, then a young advocate, lived in the fourth flat; and the fifth was possessed by John Hume, Esq. of Ninewells, who lost all his property, except a box of valuable papers.

Immediately on the discovery, the greatest exertions were made to prevent the flames from descending to the lower flats, but all proved ineffectual, and in a few hours the conflagration reached the shops, where it was not completely quenched till eight o'clock on Sunday morning, after having burnt for sixteen hours. On this occasion, all classes seemed desirous of contributing their assistance. The brewers, and their carts, laden with barrels of water, came for the supply of the engines; the Leith fire-engine was sent, and doing great execution, supplied the defect of that belonging to the city, which was out of repair, and almost useless; the soldiers of the Castle were extremely active, both in quenching the flames, and in protecting the property brought out to the street, while the magistrates superintended the proceedings in person, and even shared in the exertions of the firemen. It providentially happened that the wind blew from the west, otherwise an aged wooden tenement, immediately westward of the house in flames, must have shared the same fate. This *mako-*

gany land still stands, after seeing its stone-built neighbours twice destroyed.

It remains to be mentioned, that Buchanan's Land came in place of an antique wooden tenement, burnt in 1725, which was formerly the town-house of the Abbot and Convent of Cambuskenneth.

1779.—This year was disgraced by the violence of the mobs against the Roman Catholic inhabitants of the city. On the evening of the 2d of February a great number of people assembled at the foot of Trunk Close, and set fire to a house which they conceived to be a Popish Chapel, but which was only the residence of the bishop. This was completely consumed, notwithstanding the exertions made by a company of fencibles, and by the City-guard, to save it. On the following day, the mob plundered of its furniture, books, &c. a house in Blackfriars' Wynd, belonging to another Roman Catholic clergyman; and they afterwards broke into many shops occupied by Catholics, which they plundered of their contents.

1786.—" On Tuesday, September 12, about nine o'clock at night, a fire was discovered in a house in George's Street, of which the appearance was at first very alarming; but it was got under without doing any considerable damage. Nothing can more clearly show the excellency of the present mode of building, viz. with brick and stone partitions instead of stone as formerly, than the present instance; for though the flames raged furiously for more than an hour before any assistance was got, the fire did not spread beyond the apartment in which it began."—*Scots Mag.* vol. xlviii. p. 515.

"On the morning of Tuesday, December 12, about five o'clock, a fire was discovered in Bess Wynd, near Henderson's Stairs, at the back of the Parliament House. For a long time the appearances were truly alarming, a number of the adjacent houses being mostly composed of wood. The Lord Provost, Magistrates, and City Guard, gave immediate attendance, and by the proper attention of the people who managed the fire-engines, together with pulling down part of a tenement in Forrester's Wynd, it was happily got pretty much under about ten o'clock."—*Scots Mag.* vol. xlviii. p. 618.

By this fire,* the Parliament House, which

---

* We have heard that it was eventually put out by throwing wet cow-hides into the flames, which was

then contained the records of the kingdom, as well as the Advocates' Library, was greatly endangered. The danger was so great that the Court of Session did not meet that day. The fire was scarcely altogether extinguished for a week.

1788.—On Saturday, September 27, at eight o'clock P. M. a most alarming fire was discovered in a gentleman's house in Rose Court, immediately behind St. Andrew's Church, Edinburgh, which, in spite of the efforts of the Magistrates, military, and city-guard, together with the firemen and a numerous body of tradesmen and others, was totally consumed, together with all the furniture, and almost every thing in the house.* There was a plentiful supply of water; but no engine being to be had from nearer than the Castle-hill, it was an hour before they appeared. However, after they were got to the spot, they were so powerfully served, that the two adjoining houses, which every body thought it was impossible to save, were prevented from being burnt, al-

done at the suggestion of Mr. James Ramsay, slater to the Board of Ordnance.
* Scots Mag. vol. L. p. 514.

though a good deal damaged. "It was somewhat remarkable," say the public prints upon this occasion, " that in this, as well as in almost every similar case, the servant girls were the most useful, and exerted themselves more than the men in carrying water."

1790.—On Wednesday morning, March 16, an alarming fire broke out in the great Malting at Canonmills, which in two hours entirely consumed the building, consisting of a large barn, three granaries, and two kilns. The flames were finally got under by the exertions of the Edinburgh and Leith engines, which promptly attended. The premises were insured; and though 100 feet of wall gave way at once, no lives were lost.

Early on Sunday morning, April 18, a fire broke out in the printing-house of Messrs. Martin and Macdowall, Back Stairs, Parliament Square; which entirely consumed the same; together with a valuable stock of books and utensils. The tenement consisted of seven storeys, whereof the three uppermost, with the garret, were destroyed.

1791.—On Monday, March 28, a fire broke out in a house in Blackfriars' Wynd, being that tenement upon the east side, about forty yards down, remarkable for the following inscriptions over the door:—*Nisi Dominus Frustra*, and *Blissit be the Lord in all his Giftis:* as also, *Pax intrantibus—Salus Exeuntibus.* That tenement contained a house of ill fame, in which, it was believed, the fire originated, owing to the carelessness of its disorderly inmates. On the first alarm, the greatest apprehension was entertained for the safety of the neighbouring houses, which are much crowded together, and some of them of wood. The Lord Provost, with the city-guard and a posse of the 42d regiment, attended. Although three engines were brought to the spot, only one of them could be brought to play, the close being too narrow to admit of more. This, however, was so well wrought, that the flames were confined to the house in which they commenced. The walls of the house remain to this day. The house was insured at under £1000; but many poor families lost their all. A respectable old citizen, aged above 80, was carried out during the fire; and happily no lives were lost.

It was remarked at this time, that there had been more fires in Edinburgh during a few months, than there had been for many years before; a circumstance which would go far to prove, if the idea were not a superstitious one, that fires *come by fits*, like natural diseases or plagues, or that houses are at some periods more peculiarly inflammatory than at others.*

1795.—On the morning of the 13th of January, between twelve and one o'clock, a fire broke out in a grocer's shop at the head of Blackfriars' Wynd. As that tenement and the one immediately adjoining were of wood, the most serious consequences were apprehended. Luckily, however, by immediate assistance, and an ample supply of water, it was soon extinguished, without materially damaging any part of the building except the flat in which it began. A body of the Royal Edinburgh Volunteers attended, and gave very timeous assistance, in preserving the property of the sufferers, as well as in extinguishing the fire.

* No fewer than fifteen extensive and destructive fires occurred in England during the year 1791. The last of these was the total destruction of the Duke of Richmond's house in Spring Garden, Westminster, the floors of which were lined with iron plates, and though various other precautions had been taken to render the premises incombustible.

On the fifteenth of March, 1795, an alarming fire broke out in the printing-house of Messrs. Mundell and Son, at the foot of the Royal Bank Close, which was happily discovered in sufficient time to prevent its spreading. The damage was not very considerable.

On the fifth of June 1795, about three in the morning, a fire was discovered in the workshop of Mr. William Lamb, upholsterer, situated in Morrison's Close, High Street. On the first alarm the Magistrates attended, with a considerable body of the Royal Edinburgh Volunteers, city-guard, firemen, &c. which was soon reinforced by a party of the Scots Brigade from the Castle, owing to whose exertions in preserving order, a great quantity of valuable furniture was saved; notwithstanding which, the damage done was very considerable. One Colquhoun, a journeyman of Mr. Lamb's, was killed, and four others very much hurt, by the fall of a gable. The unfortunate person left a widow and children, for whom and other sufferers a subscription was opened.

1796.—On the morning of January 12, a fire broke out in the shop of Mr. Bowman, goldsmith, Parliament Close, which, before it was discovered, got to a great height, and was extremely alarming, from the vicinity of the premises to the Parliament House, Advocates' Library, &c. The flames were so violent, that they reached at one time to the windows of the Tolbooth Church. Mr. Bowman's shop formed the lower flat of a structure called the Goldsmiths' Hall;* the whole of which was soon consumed, along with the records, papers, &c. belonging to the Corporation of Goldsmiths. It was only by the greatest exertions of the firemen and others, that the valuable buildings adjacent were saved from destruction. The ruins of the edifice burnt down on this occasion, were not removed till the alterations of the Parliament House, &c. were begun in 1808.

* This, as well as numerous late instances, might be sufficient to point out the risk which is incurred by placing important public buildings in close neighbourhood with the shops of artizans, and the abode of a low and disorderly population. It agonises an antiquarian's heart, to think of the dangers with which the Advocates' Library is surrounded. Formerly, the lower storeys of many public buildings were let off in shops; the Exchequer, the Tolbooth, and the Council-House, were so endangered, while the very Parliament-House itself was half-filled with the stalls of tradesmen.

About twenty-six years ago* a fire took place at the head of Forrester's Wynd, Lawnmarket, by which a whole land, consisting of about seven storeys, was burnt down. The fire took place while the people were attending the afternoon sermon; and when they came from church the whole affair was over. What was very remarkable, it was observed, after the whole house was emptied by the flames, that by the side of every fire in the gable wall there was a tea-kettle; indicating, we are to suppose, that people were then in the habit of placing their kettles by the fire on going to church, in order to enjoy their evening repast immediately upon the dismissal of the congregation. It is well known that this repast was formerly called *Four-hours,* in consequence of its taking place at four o'clock afternoon.

1799.—On the first of February, about two o'clock in the morning, a fire broke out in a house at the head or western extremity of the Cowgate, south side of the street, which burnt the said house to the ground, and would pro-

---

* This was perhaps the fire of a bookbinder's shop in 1797.

bably have destroyed a wooden house adjacent, had not the wind been from the east. This fire was occasioned by a foul chimney.

1800.—On the 8th of January, the Edinburgh Sugar-house in the Canongate was completely burnt down, and most of the materials and utensils were destroyed.

On Sunday the 28th of March, the upper part of a house at the foot of Brown's Close, Lawn-market, was burnt, and a considerable deal of damage done.

1801.—On the 14th of December, a very extensive granary, belonging to the Lochrin Distillery, was discovered to be on fire. The fire-engines attended immediately; but though every possible exertion was made, the whole was burnt down. The whole was, however, insured.

1807.—On the morning of Nov. 10, between three and four o'clock, the work-shop of Mr. Francis Braidwood, upholsterer in the Pleasance, was discovered to be on fire; and before assistance could be procured, the premises were entirely consumed. The proprietor of this house was a most respectable citizen, and is remarkable for having been the first person in Edinburgh who wore shoe-tyes.

1811.—Early in the morning of Sunday the 10th of November, a fire destroyed a great part of the Exchequer Chamber in the Parliament Square, and imminently endangered the neighbouring buildings. Very great exertions being made to quench the flames, they were at length got under, though not before all the upper part of the building was destroyed. The fire was so strong, and the night so favourable for its appearance, that, to a distant beholder from the south, it seemed as if the whole of the Parliament Square were in one blaze.

1813.—On Sunday evening, the 14th of February, a most destructive and memorable fire broke out in the fourth story of Bishop's Land,* at the head of Carrubber's Close, on the

* The third flat of the Bishop's Land was formerly the residence of the Bishop of Edinburgh; and exhibited a splendid antique balcony in front, formed of brass, upon which, according to tradition, that Prelate usually stood, during the *Ridings* of the Scottish Parliament, to bless the procession.—The celebrated Viscount Melville was born in this house.

north side of the High Street. Several fire engines were kept playing upon the flames all night, and succeeded in preventing them spreading to the neighbouring houses. It was not known how this fire originated; for the family in whose house it was first seen, were all at church when it broke out. A poor woman, who had been delivered of a child the night before, had to be carried out.

The celebrated Captain Manby was present on this occasion, and suggested that the windows of the flat below that in which the flames were raging should be broken, in order to prevent them from spreading downwards. His hint was not acted upon; but it might, perhaps be tried hereafter with good effect.

On the 10th of March, about five in the morning, the General Post-Office, North Bridge, was discovered to be on fire. This was occasioned by a bucket full of ashes having been left out in a passage the preceding evening. By the prompt attendance, and active exertions of the firemen, the flames were confined to the passage and one room, and got under in less than an hour.

On the 22d of April, a fire broke out in and destroyed a house in Rattray's Close, Cowgate, occupied by Mr. Paterson, silk-dyer, and others. Several adjoining tenements were also injured. On the same day, a thatched barn, near the Grange Toll, suffered considerable damage from fire.

On the thirteenth of June, the shop of Mr. Gray, baker, south side of the Grass-market, was much injured by a fire which broke out therein, and was only suppressed with the greatest difficulty.

1814.—On Sunday morning, September 11th, a fire occurred and did a great deal of damage in a watch-maker's shop, North Bridge.

On Thursday night, the 17th of November, between 11 and 12 o'clock, a most alarming fire broke out in the hat-manufactory of Messrs. Mackay and Skirving, foot of Candlemaker Row. From the violence of the wind, which at the time blew a hurricane, the flames raged to an alarming extent till near two o'clock next morning; when by the exertions of the firemen, they were prevented from spreading, and finally got under. The property was insured.

1818.—In December, on a Saturday evening, a fire broke out in the lower flat of a house in the West Bow, which destroyed three flats, expelled ten poor families, and considerably damaged the furniture, &c. of the upper floors, but was at length got under.

1819.—On the morning of the 5th of March, a very destructive fire broke out in a row of shops on the North Bridge, east side, about the centre of the street. The alarm was given at three o'clock; and, in spite of every exertion, the whole premises were levelled with the ground at five. The buildings, being very old, principally of wood, and only two storeys in height, fell an easy prey to the flames. They were part of the houses in the Cap and Feather Close, which, with the exception of them, was completely removed to make way for the North Bridge, on the extension of the Royalty in 1767. They had obstinately kept their place there, to the disgust of all who took an interest in the appearance of this city, till fire at length rid the Magistrates of their grievous eye-sore, and made way for the handsome and uniform tenements which now occupy their place. A feeling mind could scarcely part with them, however old and ugly as they were, without regret; for they formed the last relics of the close in which the ingenious but unfortunate bard, Robert Ferguson, was born.

1821.—On the 9th of October, about midnight, a fire was discovered in the second storey of a house in the Cowgate, opposite to the Parliament Stairs, which, before effective means of prevention could be rendered, mounted rapidly upwards, and in a short time involved the whole house, from top to bottom, in a fearful conflagration. The stair, unfortunately a wooden one, very soon caught fire, and cut off the escape of a poor family in the fourth flat, consisting of a father, mother, and three children, who took the desperate resolution of leaping from the windows into the street. The father, with one child in his arms, escaped with a few bruises; but the mother, who first threw over one child, which was saved and then jumped down the dreadful height with another in her arms, was not so fortunate. She was so severely hurt, that she expired a short time after in the Infirmary. A boy, also a member of this hapless family, in jumping over, was likewise killed. This calamitous fire was supposed to have been occasioned by the imprudence of a convivial party in the second flat, who had met at a *christening*.

1832.—On the 21st of September, about eleven o'clock at night, a fire broke out in an old wooden tenement, the corner of the Lady Wynd, foot of the West Port, which, from the combustible nature of the materials, in a few minutes presented a terrific appearance. This house, which was burnt to the ground, had long been a common resort of lodgers of the lowest description, and exhibited a small placard under one of its windows, with "*Beds to Set*" written upon it, referring to wretched kips, let, we understand, at twopence per night. A great number of wretches were turned out naked into the streets; but in one of the rooms, a poor Irish labourer and two children were unhappily burnt to death. One person was roused by some neighbour-lodger, on the first alarm, and could scarcely be dragged from his pallet. He had paid his twopence, he said, and was determined to have his sleep out. However, he was soon effectually roused, and brought away.

1834.—This year has been remarkable, beyond all former years, for the number of its fires; one each month being the lowest calculation. Our limits oblige us to confine ourselves to the most remarkable only. A large printing-house in Niddry Street, belonging to Messrs. Hay & Gall, was the first property of value that suffered from the flames. Being constructed of very combustible materials, it was easily consumed; and the whole was over at about eight o'clock on Sunday morning. A vast quantity of printing materials was destroyed; and it unfortunately happened that but a small proportion was insured. Not long after this disastrous occasion, one of the new buildings on the North Bridge was almost completely destroyed. On the 24th of June, about one in the morning, a most alarming fire broke out in a low tippling-house, at the head of the Royal Bank Close, (first below the High Church,) which, after burning the whole tenement in which it commenced, so that it fell, communicated with the adjacent house to the westward, and did not stop till it had devastated the half of the east side of the Parliament Square. The afternoon of Thursday was far advanced before the fury of the flames received any sensible check, and the engines continued to play upon the smoking ruins, at intervals, the three following days. To the great surprise of all who witnessed this dreadful calamity, the loss of life was confined to that of one individual, Alexander Chalmers, a town-officer, who was so scorched in endeavouring to save some papers, that he died, on the 27th, in the Infirmary. By this fire was laid waste a scene that could not have been pointed out without exciting a lively interest,—the cellar in which the celebrated Scottish wit, poet, and physician, Archibald Pitcairn, used to pass his convivial hours, upwards of a century ago. The entry to this low and dark receptacle was exactly opposite to the eastern window of St. Giles's, and descended from the piazzas which once made this part of the town so remarkable, as being the last piece of building which retained those long abrogated nuisances, in former times universal in the High Street. This cellar was the *Groping Office* which he celebrates in his "*Poemata*," and was so called on account of people having to grope their way along its dark and tortuous passages. In the fourth flat of the same *land*, lived, about fifty or sixty years ago, Lord Auchinleck, father of James Boswell, the amiable and esteemed biographer of Johnson. This fire was considered the most extensive and destructive that had happened since that of 1700; but another shortly after occurred in its immediate neighbourhood, which surpassed both of these.

GREAT FIRE OF NOVEMBER, 1824.

On the evening of Monday the fifteenth of November, at a little before ten o'clock, the alarm of "Fire!" was given in the High Street, and soon spread through the whole city. Crowds of people immediately hurried to the spot, and beheld the smoke issuing from the second flat of a house at the head of the Old Assembly Close, occupied by Messrs. Kirkwood and Sons, copper-plate printers. The upper part of this tenement, which consisted of six storeys in height, and formed the eastern wing or division of one large uniform pile of building, was, about eleven o'clock, completely involved in the flames.

Between ten and eleven several fire-engines arrived on the spot, but it was some time later before any water was discharged. A party of soldiers to line the street, and another party with a fire-engine, were sent from the Castle, and performed their duty with all the regularity and discretion usually observed in disciplined soldiers. The Sheriff, Lord Provost, and Bailies also attended, and many other high official personages engaged themselves actively; but the want of an experienced director, to regulate and give effect to the operations, was severely felt, and afterwards generally acknowledged.

The wind at this time was extremely gentle, and came from the south-west, so that the flames which issued from the windows were at first directed towards the front of the eastern tenement, which was for some time considerably endangered. But this house being separated by a strong gable, and, moreover, being of the best modern construction, resisted the flames, though the leaden pipe between the tenements, through which the rain descended from the roof to the street, was completely melted away. The two *lands* to the westward were not, however, so fortunate. The fire communicated to them from behind, where, from the narrowness of the close, it was impossible to ply an engine; and about twelve o'clock, the flames had spread from house to house, till all that pile of building, consisting of three tenements, between Borthwick's close and the modern tenement alluded to, was involved in one stupendous blaze.

The greatest fears were now entertained for the Courant Office, a tall narrow *land* of better construction than the burning tenement; and, about two o'clock, while many persons connected with this establishment were endeavouring to save papers, books, &c. the fire communicated to the upper flat. At this juncture, several enterprising individuals ascended to the roof of the large tenement west of the Courant Office, where, seeing that they could easily command the roof of that edifice from the high over-topping gable on which they stood, they bawled down to the firemen on the street for a pipe to be employed in that manner. This, however, they were nearly an hour in procuring, during which time the progress of the flames had almost made their project hopeless. And no sooner had the firemen attended to their demands than the whole attempt was rendered vain by the inefficiency of the pipe, which was most unfortunately broken in several places: otherwise, we have every reason to believe, the Courant office might have been saved, as well as all that extensive range of property down the Old Fish-market and Assembly Closes, to which it was the means of communicating the flames.

While the three front tenements were yielding to destruction, the night was calm and serene, and the sparks sent forth by the flames rose high into the air, like embers shot from the crater of a volcano. Their appearance was like the thickest *drift* of a snow-storm,—an image that was suggested to the fancy of many of the by-standers; and the writer of this narrative was particularly amused by hearing a native of Aberdeenshire exclaim, " See the *red snaw!*" Showers of burning flakes fell upon the dense assembled crowd, to the great damage of their clothes, and, at a moment of peculiar danger, caused a rush down the street, which gave the most serious alarm to those at a distance.

Many of the chimneys in the neighbourhood were set on fire by these embers; and it was curious to observe here and there, issuing from the picturesque peaks of the houses, a small stream of flame, rendered pale and light by the intensity of the greater conflagration against which it was relieved. The Tron Church was for a considerable time completely enveloped in these dangerous showers of flakes; and we remember of imagining, as a possible occurrence, the disastrous fate which next day befell that building, though the succeeding thought was sufficient to lull our unexpressed and momentary fears in the security of our fellow-citizens. A little after one o'clock, an alarm of fire was given from the house opposite to those destroyed; but after a short suspense of horror and dismay, it was found to be only a chimney.

Shortly after this period, the night began to change its character, and the wind, accompanied with rain, rose in sudden and fitful gusts.

About five o'clock, the fire of the Courant Office had proceeded so far down the building, that the pinnacle and upper part of the front wall fell inwards, when the flames burst into the middle of the street; and shortly afterwards another portion fell. The strong gable of the high tenement to the west successfully resisted the fire; but the line of building, connecting with the Courant Office behind, was speedily destroyed, and the adjoining house, down the Old Fish-market Close, occupied by Mr. Abraham Thomson, book-binder, (lately destroyed by fire, and rebuilt in 1824,) was, by the fall of a gable, partially crushed to the ground. The back tenements at the upper extremities of Borthwick's and the Old Assembly Closes, were also entirely consumed, including the Old Assembly Hall, then occupied as a warehouse by Messrs. Bell & Bradfute, booksellers. This was perhaps the most massy, and certainly not the least stupendous pile of building in the city, and in former times was inhabited by people of the greatest distinction*. Great part of the southern *land* fell to the ground, while a tall pile of sidewall fell over upon the tenement on the opposite side of the close, where it remained in an inclined posture for a few days.

By nine o'clock, on the morning of Tuesday, the fire had considerably abated, and by mid-day it seemed to be nearly subdued; but while the consternation into which the neighbourhood was thrown by the circumstances related, was beginning to subside, the fears of all were revived by the appearance of another sudden and unexpected calamity in a different quarter.

A little before twelve o'clock, the word was given that the Tron Church † was on fire!

---

* This *land* had a magnificent *scale-stair*, a sure test of respectability in old Edinburgh mansions. In the third flat, and southern division of the *land*, lived Lord Royston, a distinguished Judge, (son of the celebrated first Earl of Cromarty,) who died here in 1744.

† The Tron-Church was begun to be built in the year 1637, when the magistrates also intended to erect a similar structure in the Castle-hill Street, the plan of which was, however, laid aside from deficiency of funds. The Castle-hill church was to have stood upon the site of the present reservoir, which edifice was placed upon

The agitation and alarm communicated to every part of the town by this intelligence, it is impossible to describe. This edifice, being separated by the breadth of a street from every other building, and at the distance of nearly two hundred yards from the former conflagration, was the last place where the flames might have been expected to revive. Moreover,

its neglected foundation. The Tron-Church was so named from its vicinity to the Trone, or place for public weighing of merchandize. The inscription upon the building bears date 1641; but the church was not fit for the reception of a congregation till 1647, nor was it properly roofed in till 1663. In 1673, a bell was put up; and, five years thereafter, a clock was procured, (being that which formerly adorned the Weighhouse,) and also placed in the steeple. Robert Fergusson's humorous address to this bell is well known. Were he now alive, he might write its elegy; for never again will its discordant tones summon lazy and unwilling writers' clerks to their work—the recent fire having completely melted it away. In 1789, when this part of the city underwent a great alteration, by the opening up of the South Bridge, the houses which before that period were contiguous to the Church, were taken away, and its walls were entirely rebuilt, except that of the northern front. It was opened for divine service, for the first time after these improvements, October 25, 1789.

there was something sacred in its character as a church, which, in every body's idea, was supposed to exempt it from the attack of any such calamity. In the excitement of the moment, numbers breathed within themselves, or half-expressed, the belief which they entertained, that it was "*judgment-like!*" and even the most unconcerned and profligate persons found themselves incapable of beholding this terrific scene with indifference. It was supposed that some of the flying brands had found their way into the tower, by a window, usually furnished with pent-house boards, which had been blown inwards by the hurricane early in the morning; and that these, being fanned into a flame, produced the dreadful catastrophe. On the first alarm, the firemen, spent as they were with the exertions of the morning, hurried to the spot, where they found a small flame issuing from the south-west corner of the ballustrade (formed of wood,) which surmounts the tower. Some, by means of long ladders, reached the roof of the church, from whence they were enabled occasionally to repel the appearance of the flame as it issued from various parts of the steeple. But their exertions were vain and ineffectual, in putting a stop to the devastation which was evidently raging in the interior of the building; and, in a short time, the whole conical or rather pyramidal superstructure, entirely of wood, cased in lead, was in a blaze, the flames ascending to the top with the greatest fury, and presenting a spectacle singularly terrific and sublime. The weathercock stood for a long time pre-eminent, like a phoenix springing upward from the flame; but at length it began to veer, and after reeling for a moment, fell, along with the spire, towards the east, with a tremendous crash. The machinery of the clock was now distinctly visible through the apertures of the tower, and gleamed as in a furnace. The clock upon the eastern side of the tower appears to have been earlier affected than the rest; for the *hands* had stopped at twenty minutes to twelve, while the western dial-plate presented them at a quarter to one. The fire-men, who had stood near the scene of danger longer than was judged safe by the crowd, now retired; but, after the spire had fallen, they again ascended to the roof, and endeavoured to save the body of the church, when a mass of burning rafters fell among them, happily without doing any injury. It *is* probable that the church would have also been consumed, but for the seasonable arrival of Deacon Field, an enterprising and most active individual, with a powerful engine belonging to the Board of Ordnance, by means of which the flames were not only confined to the steeple, but were at length got completely under. By this destructive event, the Tron Church steeple was scathed, and emptied of all its internal furniture, so that it resembled nothing so much as the ruined tower of some aged and dilapidated abbey.

After the tragical scenes above described, it was naturally hoped that the calamities of Edinburgh were for the present at an end. But, at ten o'clock at night, a new alarm was given of a fire having broken out in the Parliament Square. It began in the top-storey of that immense pile of building on the south side of the Square, formerly pointed out to strangers as the highest in Edinburgh, being at the back part, which overlooked the Cowgate, eleven storeys in height. From the situation of this building, so far to windward of the scene of the former fire, it was judged impossible that the one could have been the cause of the other. This was a perfectly distinct conflagration, and had the effect of impressing people with an idea that Heaven was beginning to afflict them with a series of terrific and destructive calamities. The fire speedily descended from the place where it broke out to the chambers of Mr. Guthrie Wright, Auditor of the Court of Session, to the Jury-Court Rooms, and downwards to the depths of the building below. The houses in this quarter presented at first a most afflicting scene. From windows at a great height the inhabitants busied themselves in tossing over their furniture, and even loose papers, the greater part of which were of course destroyed. The Parliament Square and St. Giles' resounded with awful echoes; the torches of the firemen below threw up a horrid light upon the tall surrounding buildings; and as the flames proceeded, volumes of smoke and embers were driven eastward in violent and appalling career across the Old Town. From behind, the scene was, if possible, more fearful; for the height of the buildings in which the flames raged, was such, that they seemed beyond the reach of human exertions, and threatened a wide-spread district beneath with impending ruin. Any attempt to save this tenement was speedily rendered vain, and the attention of the firemen was very properly directed to the valuable buildings adjacent upon the west, by which means they were happily saved. "The fire,* however, spread resistlessly in the opposite direction. The roof of the adjoining house on the east side of the Square first appeared in a flame, and the fire afterwards broke out in the angle towards the Square from the windows and shopdoors. From these, it ascended in one continuous blaze up the front of the building; and about five o'clock in the morning, all the eastern side of the Square, not consumed by the recent fire, [of June last,] presented one huge burning tower, the beams crashing and falling inwards, and every opening and window pouring forth flame. The scene was now awfully grand; and could we have divested ourselves of the thoughts of the losses, and hardships, and ruin, which attended the progress of the conflagration, we could not have been placed in a situation where we could have derived such a portion of sublime enjoyment. The whole horizon was completely enveloped in lurid flame. The consternation, the daring, the suspense, the fear, that sat upon different faces, seemed each appropriately lighted up to express their several emotions the more vividly. The dusky faces of the firemen gleam-

* Edinburgh Evening Courant, Nov. 18, 1824.

ed from under their caps, as their heads were raised with each repeated stroke of the engine; and the very element by which they endeavoured to extinguish the conflagration, seemed itself a stream of liquid fire. The clattering of the horses' hoofs, and the light reflected from their riders' swords, added a kind of martial terror to the scene; and when we beheld the whole surrounded either with burning piles, or with edifices that reflected a light more fearful than even that which was thrown upon them, we felt a thrill of mingled fear and admiration. The County Hall, at one time, appeared like a palace of light; and the venerable steeple of St. Giles' reared itself amidst the bright flames, like a spectre awakened to behold the fall and ruin of the devoted city."

By eight o'clock the violence of the flames had abated; the fire had indeed burnt out, and at that period the interior walls of the south-east angle fell upon the front wall, and precipitated them into the square, with a crash that was tremendous, and a cloud of dust that darkened the atmosphere. Here several persons were severely hurt. The only part of the old buildings in the square then remaining, was the *land* adjoining the Exchequer buildings—a fabric which, it is remarkable, also survived the fire of 1700. During the night, that part of the Old Town to the eastward of the conflagration was exposed to an incessant shower of sparks and flaming brands.* These again set fire to the buildings in the rear of the High Street, where the flames broke out with such violence, that the greatest anxiety prevailed for the safety of the whole of the Old Town, no part of which was now considered beyond the reach of the wide-spreading calamity. Here the most melancholy accidents happened, in one of which Mr. Braidwood, director of the engines, nearly lost his life; but here, we rejoice to add, the great fire of 1824 at length terminated. During the day, frequent alarms were given in other places, originating principally in chimneys ignited by burning embers. One broke out in a house in Carrubber's Close, but was soon got under. Towards the evening a heavy shower of rain helped to extinguish the embers lodged in the tops of the houses; prior to which, a proclamation was issued by the

* Burning fragments fell at the Easter Road Toll-Bar, about a mile and a half from the scene of conflagration.

Magistrates, recommending a general inspection of the house-tops, and the stationing of watches thereon.

From three to four hundred families were burnt out by this dreadful calamity; and there was not a close nor a retired corner near the place, but what was crowded with the wrecks of their humble property. Many of the sufferers received shelter in Queensberry House, Canongate, where their wants were attended to by the humane and by the Magistrates.

We hastily add a few *memorabilia* of this disastrous occasion.

The Lord Advocate exerted himself with great activity, and wrought for some time even at the engines. On such an occasion all distinction of ranks was lost, and one working man ventured to slap his Lordship heartily on the back, exclaiming, " Weel done, my Lord!" It is not perhaps generally known that Sir William Rae was born in the house which he thus exerted himself in saving—viz. in the third flat of the centre tenement at the head of the Old Assembly Close. Here, at the time when the Old Town was alike the habitation of the upper and the lower ranks, his father, David Rae (afterwards Lord Eskgrove) resided. A venerable W. S. informs us, that he was in Lord Eskgrove's house when the North Bridge fell. The crash was louder than thunder, and alarmed all present. Lord E. started up in a distracted manner, apprehending some dreadful accident, and ran out, crying for his children, and could not be pacified till he found them safe.

When the flames were at the highest on Monday night, the whole crowd seemed struck with silent wonder. One person near us motioned to his companion that he wished to go home, which the other did not seem willing to assent to; and he strongly urged that *the fire was well worth seeing.* "Aye," said the first speaker, with a feeling that did him honour, " if it were a *banefire*," (bonfire.)

When the flames were raging in one of the closes, a poor Irishman descended from a miserable garret, and, wringing his hands in despair, cried out that he was ruined and undone, all that he had in the world being nearly within reach of the flames. Some of the crowd, whose compassion he excited, ran up the stair to his wretched abode, where they found nothing but a heap of straw in a corner of the room and a ricketty chair. This nearly raised a laugh among the by-standers; but the Irishman, without altering his tone, exclaimed, "Seoul! gentlemen, is it not my all!"

The superstitions which we have recorded respecting the fire of 1700, almost find a parallel in some which we heard expressed among the crowd on this occasion. One old woman engaged in watching a pile of furniture at the head of the College Wynd, we overheard uttering to a neighbour her belief that the whole calamity was a judgment in consequence of the late Musical Festival. This was also the sentiment of the people of Corstorphine, who saw the conflagration at a distance of three miles. And many other such ideas were entertained upon the subject.—At Berwick, a report prevailed, that the whole town, Old and New, was destroyed!

The following was, as nearly as could be ascertained, the extent of the mischief.— Along the front of the High Street there were destroyed four lands of six storeys each, besides the sunk storeys; from these down towards the Cowgate by Conn's Close, two wooden lands; in the Old Assembly Close, four lands of six or seven storeys; six smaller tenements in Borthwick's Close; four lands of six storeys in the Old Fishmarket Close. Downwards, nearly as far as the Cowgate, nothing was to be seen but frightful heaps of ruin, to which all approach was rendered highly dangerous, by the walls which were left standing in different places, but in an extremely tottering condition. Along the front of the Parliament Square, four double lands, of from seven to eleven storeys each, were destroyed. The appearance of the back-wall of the enormous fabric, which occupied the south-east angle of the square, was strikingly sublime, from its enormous height of nine stories, and from its being left without any support, or any connection with its former front. It was difficult to estimate the number of families that were rendered houseless by this great calamity. But when we consider the height of some of the buildings, and the density of the population in this quarter, six or seven families being sometimes crowded together into one floor, the number could not fall short of 250; indeed we have little doubt that if an accurate calculation could have been made, they might have been found to exceed that number. Such a scene of calamity as this is seldom paralleled in the annals of domestic life. Besides those buildings utterly destroyed by the fire, a great deal of property was damaged by the falling of the burning ruins, and much was destroyed or lost in the removals occasioned by the general alarm; for such was the threatening appearance of the fire on Wednesday morning, that not only in the Cowgate, but even in Hunter's Square and Blair Street, many individuals removed their most valuable furniture. On the South Bridge, and other parts in the direction of the thick showers of fire then falling, persons were stationed on the roofs of most of the houses, to sweep off the burning embers as they fell, and occasionally to pour water on the roofs. About eleven o'clock on Tuesday morning, a portion of the building occupied by the Courant Office, immediately over the premises of Mr. Rymer, gave way, at a moment when unfortunately three boys were in it. One of them, more lucky than the others, made his escape. The rubbish, in falling, shut the two folding doors, just so as to entrap the second, who was released from his perilous situation by the tearing up of the door; his right foot seemed to be severely hurt. The third boy was totally overwhelmed with the rubbish, from whence his miserable father recovered his mutilated corpse on Thursday morning. Besides those individuals who were carried to the Royal Infirmary, many received hurts, who were taken charge of by their friends; and a dragoon, who was much wounded, was carried to the Castle.

About 12 noon on Saturday, the south gable in the Parliament Square was partially brought down *inwards;* and the sappers and miners having made the necessary preparations, the mines were fired at a few minutes before one o'clock. The immense pile on the east side of the Square, which threatened destruction to the Police Office and the other tenements below, also fell *inwards,* as predicted by Captain Head. At this time, one solitary pile of the southern gable (being nearly the south-east corner of the Square) remained. Here the greatest danger was apprehended, and here also the greatest danger was avoided. When the skeleton, for such in truth it appeared, of the loftiest range of buildings in Edinburgh fell, a trifling portion of it struck the lower grounds—and one or two small houses of little value were injured. The sinking of the wall on the eastern side of the Square was truly magnificent. A part of it sunk down immediately after the mine was sprung, and the remainder in two successive fragments, followed with such pauses only as